THE
Bedside
BOOK

D1464147

DAVID SHORT

THE BEDSIDE BOOK

Acknowledgments

The compiler acknowledges the authors and editors of previous collections of hymns and prayers, particularly William Barclay's Prayers for Help and Healing, W.R. Mackay's In Time of Need, Prayers of Peter Marshall, and Prayers for Health and Healing (SPCK).

I am obliged to Christian Education for permission to reproduce the prayer by Michael Walker, included on Day 16; to CopyCare for licence to use the hymns by Melody Green (Day 16), Brian Doerksen (Day 24), Edward Turney (Day 28), and T.W. Maltby (Day 1); to Bucks Music to use the hymn by Alfred B. Smith and Eugene Clarke (Day 6); to Crusade for World Revival for permission to use the prayer from Hope Eternal by Selwyn Hughes (Day 23); to Bishop Timothy Dudley-Smith for permission to use his hymn Safe in the shadow of the Lord (Day 8); to Highland Books for permission to quote the prayer by John Gunstone (Day 27); to Kingsway Communications Ltd for permission to use the hymn Father I place into your hands by Jenny Hewer (Day 22) and the hymn O the joy of your forgiveness by Dave Bilbrough (Day 31); to Make Way Music for permission to include the verses of hymns by Graham Kendrick reproduced on Days 3 and 11; and to SPCK for permission to quote the prayer by George Appleton which appears on Day 4.

I am indebted to a number of friends for constructive criticism; notably Renée Cowan, Nicholas Gray, Judy Short, and Graham and Hazel Black, and to The Drummond Trust, 3 Pitt Terrace, Stirling for their financial assistance.

First edition 2003
This edition reprinted 2012
ISBN 0 948643 47 1
Published by Chapter House Ltd
47 Purdon Street
Glasgow G11 6AF
0141 337 6529

Scripture quotations taken from
The Holy Bible,
New International Version
Copyright 1973, 1978, 1984 by
International Bible Society
Used by permission of Hodder &
Stoughton Ltd.

The Holy Bible,
New King James Version
Copyright 1982
by Thomas Nelson, Inc.

CONTENTS

WHAT THIS BOOK OFFERS

There is nothing like a spell in hospital, or an unexpected change of life, to focus one's mind on God and the things that really matter.

In my practice as a hospital doctor, I discovered a little book of Scripture and prayers and familiar hymns which was much appreciated by my patients. It was called the 'Hospital Bedside Book', compiled by Duncan Heriot. Sadly, that book is now out of print. This new, revised, book is the result of years of reading and reflection enriched by the experience of going through four operations. I well remember the joy and comfort I felt when my son, a medical student at that time, visited me after one major operation which was followed by a serious complication. He brought me a Bible verse from the Epistle to the Hebrews which tells us that in Jesus we have someone who completely understands our weaknesses.

The Bedside Book offers a selection of small, tasty, spiritual snacks, particularly for those confined to hospital or some other unfamiliar environment. It majors on the Bible, God's Word, because this comes with divine authority. It is relevant to the whole spectrum of human need, and is never out of date. Moreover, the Bible has an unsurpassed track record of bringing help and comfort to all ages and conditions. Many can say with the Psalmist: "Your Word is a lamp to my feet and a light for my path... ... Oh, how I love your law! I meditate on it all day long."

The Scripture passages I have chosen are brief, but profound in meaning. May I suggest reading a short section slowly and thoughtfully, and then pausing to think about it. In a surprisingly short time you will find that you have stored many helpful thoughts in your mind, and provided yourself with an inner strength of spirit.

I have included hymns because the best ones are an expression of Scripture truths in an easily memorisable form. When God wanted the children of Israel to commit his teaching to memory, he instructed Moses to embody it in a hymn. Since they have been a source of blessing to God's people down the ages, I have included a few of the great hymns from earlier centuries.

I have also included prayers. These are are designed as an aid rather than a substitute for your own personal prayers. It is important to remember that prayer is simply talking to an unseen but ever-present and loving Father. Besides bringing him our needs, it is good if we can tell him how much he means to us, how sorry we are for our shortcomings and thank him for the good things he has given us. We should also take time, however hard our circumstances, to pray for others. The main ingredients of prayer are summed up in the acronym ACTS - adoration, confession, thanksgiving, supplication.

Several of the prayers I have chosen were composed by Christians from earlier ages. Their language may sound strange to modern ears, but they have a timeless, powerful resonance. Unattributed prayers are either from an unknown source or have been supplied by the compiler of the Hospital Bedside Book or the compiler of the present volume.

Permission to quote scriptures, hymns and prayers has been carefully sought. If any copyright has been infringed, the compiler craves forgiveness in view of the purpose for which the book has been produced.

David Short

HOW TO GET THE MAXIMUM VALUE FROM THE MEDITATIONS

Read a few lines at a time, slowly and thoughtfully;
then lie back and meditate on them. Say to yourself:

> I am here by God's appointment.
>
> I am here in God's keeping.
>
> I am here under His training.
>
> I am here for His time.

Listen for God's voice speaking into your mind, and respond
appropriately, whether in thankfulness or repentance or obedience.

**A suggested
prayer before reading**

O Lord, Heavenly Father,
in whom is the fullness of light
and wisdom:
enlighten my mind by your
Holy Spirit,
and give me grace to receive
your Word with reverence and
humility,
without which no one can
understand your truth;
for Christ's sake.
Amen.

from John Calvin

The Lord's Prayer

Our Father in heaven,
hallowed be your name,
your kingdom come,
your will be done,
on earth as in heaven.
Give us today our daily bread.
Forgive us our sins as
we forgive those who sin
against us.
Lead us not into temptation
but deliver us from evil.
For the kingdom, the power,
and the glory are yours
now and forever.
Amen.

DAY 1

The Lord is my shepherd, I shall not want.

I am the good shepherd; I know my sheep and my sheep know me - just as the Father knows me and I know the Father - and I lay down my life for the sheep. I have other sheep that are not of this sheep pen. I must bring them also. They too will listen to my voice, and there shall be one flock and one shepherd. The reason my Father loves me is that I lay down my life - only to take it up again. No-one takes it from me, but I lay it down of my own accord. I have authority to lay it down and authority to take it up again. This command I received from my Father. My sheep listen to my voice; I know them, and they follow me. I give them eternal life, and they shall never perish: no-one can snatch them out of my hand. My Father, who has given them to me, is greater than all; no-one can snatch them out of my Father's hand. I and the Father are one.

Christ is the answer to my every need;
Christ is the answer, he is my friend indeed.
Problems of life my spirit may assail,
With Christ my Saviour I need never fail,
For Christ is the answer to my need.

PRAYERS

In the morning
Thou, O Christ, art all I want; more than all in Thee I find.
Raise the fallen, cheer the faint,
Heal the sick, and lead the blind:
Just and holy is Thy name, I am all unrighteousness;
False and full of sin I am,
Thou art full of truth and grace.

Plenteous grace with Thee is found, grace to cover all my sin;
Let the healing streams abound,
Make and keep me pure within:
Thou of life the fountain art, freely let me take of Thee,
Spring Thou up within my heart, rise to all eternity.

Charles Wesley

In the evening
Ere I sleep, for every favour this day showed by my God,
I will bless my Saviour.

O my God what shall I render to Thy name,
still the same,
Merciful and tender.

Thou hast ordered all my goings in Thy way,
heard me pray,
Sanctified my doings.

John Cennick

DAY 2

**He guides the humble in what is right and
teaches them his way.**

DAILY READING *From John 15*

I am the true vine, and my Father is the vinedresser. Every branch in me that does not bear fruit he takes away; and every branch that bears fruit he prunes, that it may bear more fruit. I am the vine, you are the branches. He who abides in me and I in him, bears much fruit; for without me you can do nothing. If you abide in me and my words abide in you, you will ask what you desire, and it shall be done for you. By this my Father is glorified, that you bear much fruit; so you will be my disciples. If you keep my commandments, you will abide in my love, just as I have kept my Father's commands and abide in his love. These things I have spoken to you that my joy may remain in you, and that your joy may be full. This is my commandment,that you love one another as I have loved you. Greater love has no one than this, than to lay down one's life for his friends. You are my friends if you do whatever I command you.

I need Thee every hour, most gracious Lord;
No tender voice like Thine can peace afford.

I need Thee, O I need Thee,
every hour I need Thee;
O bless me now my Saviour; I come to Thee.

I need Thee every hour; teach me Thy will,
And Thy rich promises in me fulfil.

PRAYERS

In the morning
Teach me Thy way, O Lord, teach me Thy way!
Thy gracious aid afford, teach me Thy way!
Help me to walk aright, more by faith, less by sight;
Lead me with heavenly light: teach me Thy way!

When doubts and fears arise, teach me Thy way!
When storms o'erspread the skies, teach me Thy way!
Shine through the cloud and rain, through sorrow,
toil and pain;
Make Thou my pathway plain: teach me Thy way!

Benjamin Mansell Ramsey

In the evening
Lead kindly Light, amid the encircling gloom, lead Thou me on;
The night is dark, and I am far from home; lead Thou me on.
Keep Thou my feet; I do not ask to see the distant scene;
one step enough for me.

Cardinal Newman

O God, thank you for everything that has been done for
me by anyone today, and thank you for those who have
come to visit me.
Thank you for everything that has helped me to become more
healthy in body, and more cheerful and contented in mind.

William Barclay

11

DAY 3

Trials have come so that your faith may
be proved genuine.

DAILY READING *From 1 Peter 1*

Blessed be the God and Father of our Lord Jesus Christ, who according to his abundant mercy has begotten us again to a living hope through the resurrection of Jesus Christ from the dead, to an inheritance incorruptible and undefiled and that does not fade away, reserved in heaven for you, who are kept by the power of God through faith for salvation ready to be revealed in the last time. In this you greatly rejoice, though now for a little while, if need be, you have been grieved by various trials, that the genuineness of your faith, being much more precious than gold that perishes, though it is tested by fire, may be found to praise, honour and glory at the revelation of Jesus Christ, whom having not seen you love. Though now you do not see him, yet believing, you rejoice with joy inexpressible and full of glory, receiving the end of your faith - the salvation of your souls.

Fear not, I am with you, oh, be not dismayed;
I, I am your God and will still give you aid;
I'll strengthen you, help you, and cause you to stand,
Upheld by my righteous, omnipotent hand.

When through fiery trials your pathway shall lie,
My grace all-sufficient shall be your supply;
The flame shall not hurt you; I only design
Your dross to consume, and your gold to refine.

12

PRAYERS

In the morning
O merciful God, be Thou now unto me a strong tower
of defence, I humbly entreat Thee.
Give me grace to await Thy pleasure,
and patiently bear what Thou doest unto me;
nothing doubting or mistrusting Thy goodness towards me;
for Thou knowest what is good for me better than I do.
Therefore do with me in all things what Thou wilt;
only arm me, I beseech Thee, with Thine armour,
that I may stand fast;
above all things, taking to me the shield of faith;
praying always that I may refer myself wholly to Thy will,
abiding Thy pleasure and comforting myself in those
troubles which it shall please Thee to send me,
seeing such troubles are profitable for me;
and I am assuredly persuaded that all Thou doest cannot
but be well; and unto Thee be all honour and glory.

Lady Jane Grey

In the evening
Be present, O merciful God, and protect us through the
silent hours of this night, so that we who are sick and
weary may rest untroubled and unafraid; through Jesus
Christ our Lord.

Ancient Collect

DAY 4

He knows the way that I take; when he has tested me,
I shall come forth as gold.

DAILY READING *From 2 Corinthians 4 and 5*

Though outwardly we are wasting away, yet inwardly we are being renewed day by day. So we fix our eyes not on what is seen, but on what is unseen. For what is seen is temporary, but what is unseen is eternal. Now we know that if the earthly tent we live in is destroyed, we have a building from God, an eternal house in heaven, not built by human hands. It is God who has made us for this very purpose and has given us the Spirit as a deposit, guaranteeing what is to come. We live by faith, not by sight. So we make it our goal to please him. For we must all appear before the judgment seat of Christ, that each one may receive what is due to him for the things done while in the body, whether good or bad.

Be still, my soul: The Lord is on Thy side;
bear patiently the cross of grief or pain;
Leave to Thy God to order and provide;
in every change He faithful will remain.
Be still, my soul: Thy best Thy heavenly Friend
through thorny ways leads to a joyful end.

PRAYERS

In the morning

I thank you, Father, that although you are concerned
about all that goes on in the universe, your eye is on me,
and you never for a moment lose sight of me.

I thank you too that my trials and difficulties are not
purposeless, and that your Word tells us that you have
prepared for those who love you such things as pass
our understanding.

I thank you that you have a wonderful future in store for
me, and that all the circumstances through which I am
passing, however disturbing, are preparing me for
ultimate glory.

I pray that as a result of my experiences, I may be able
to understand and help others who are facing
similar difficulties.

In the evening

Lord Jesus Christ, who didst hear the prayer of thy two
disciples and didst abide with them at eventide.

Abide, we pray thee with all people in the evening of life.
Make thyself known to them, and let thy light shine upon
their path; and whenever they shall pass through the
valley of the shadow of death, be with them unto the end;
through Jesus Christ our Lord.

George Appleton

DAY 5

As for God, his way is perfect.

DAILY READING *From Luke 11*

Ask and it will be given to you; seek and you will find; knock and the door will be opened to you. For everyone who asks receives; he who seeks finds; and to him who knocks, the door will be opened. Which of you fathers, if your son asks for a fish, will give him a snake instead? Or if he asks for an egg, will give him a scorpion? If you then, though you are evil, know how to give good gifts to your children, how much more will your Father in heaven give the Holy Spirit to those who ask him.

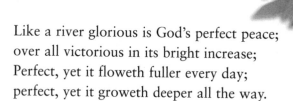

Like a river glorious is God's perfect peace;
over all victorious in its bright increase;
Perfect, yet it floweth fuller every day;
perfect, yet it groweth deeper all the way.

Stayed upon Jehovah hearts are fully blest;
finding, as he promised, perfect peace and rest.

PRAYERS

In the morning
Have Thine own way, Lord, have Thine own way:
Thou art the potter, I am the clay;
Mould me and make me after Thy will,
While I am waiting, yielded and still.

Adelaide Addison Pollard

O God, my Father, I thank you that you are utterly
trustworthy and that you do not put your children
through needless pain or distress. I pray for a sense of
serenity and total relaxation in your all-secure and loving
arms. Give me confidence and peace as I commit myself
to you today.

In the evening
Before I sleep I remember before you all the people I
love and now, in the silence, I say their names to
you. I remember before you all the people who are
sad and lonely, old and forgotten, poor and hungry
and cold, in pain of body and in distress of mind.
Bless all who specially need your blessing, and bless
me too, and make this a good night for me.
This I ask for your love's sake.

William Barclay

DAY 6

My times are in your hands.

DAILY READING *From Psalm 90*

Lord, you have been our dwelling-place throughout all generations. Before the mountains were brought forth, or ever you had formed the earth and the world, even from everlasting to everlasting you are God. You turn men to destruction, and say, "Return, O children of men." For a thousand years in your sight are like yesterday when it is past, and like a watch in the night. Teach us to number our days, that we may gain a heart of wisdom. Oh, satisfy us early with your mercy, that we may rejoice and be glad all our days! Make us glad according to the days in which you have afflicted us, the years in which we have seen evil. Let your work appear to your servants, and your glory to their children. And let the beauty of the Lord our God be upon us, and establish the work of our hands for us; yes, establish the work of our hands.

I do not know what lies ahead, the way I cannot see;
Yet one stands near to be my guide, he'll show the way to me:

I know who holds the future, and he'll guide me with his hand;
With God things don't just happen, everything by him is planned.
So, as I face tomorrow, with its problems large and small,
I'll trust the God of miracles, give to him my all.

PRAYERS

In the morning

O God our Father, what is before us, we know not, but this we do know, that all things are ordered with unerring wisdom and unbounded love, by Thee our God, who art love. Grant us in all things to see Thy hand; through Jesus Christ our Lord, Amen.

Charles Simeon

Father, I thank you that if I stay where I am, you are with me and if I have to move somewhere else you, the Good Shepherd, will go on ahead of me. Give me, I pray, a serene acceptance of this fact. I am grateful to know that my times are, indeed, in your hands. Help me to wait patiently and confidently for your time.

In the evening

God, my Father, I thank you for the assurance of your unfailing love and strength. Help me to rest on you. I commend to your care also those who care for me, and my loved ones.

I will lay me down in peace and sleep: for Thou, Lord, only makest me to dwell in safety.

Psalm 3

DAY 7

Rest in the Lord and wait patiently for him.

DAILY READING *From Isaiah 40*

Behold, the Lord God shall come with a strong hand, and his arm shall rule for him; Behold, his reward is with him and his work before him. He will feed his flock like a shepherd: he will gather the lambs with his arm, and carry them in his bosom, and gently lead those that are with young. Have you not known? Have you not heard? The everlasting God, the Lord, the creator of the ends of the earth, neither faints nor is weary, his understanding is unsearchable. He gives power to the weak, and to those who have no might he increases strength. Even the youths shall faint and be weary, and the young men shall utterly fall, but those who wait on the Lord shall renew their strength; they shall mount up with wings like eagles, they shall run and not be weary, they shall walk and not faint.

All my hope on God is founded;
He doth still my trust renew;
Me through change and chance He guideth,
only good and only true
God unknown, He alone calls my heart to be His own.

PRAYERS

In the morning

Into Thy hands, O God, we commend ourselves and all who are dear to us this day. Let the gift of Thy special presence be with us even unto its close. Grant us never to lose sight of Thee all the day long, so that at eventide we may again give thanks unto Thee; through Jesus Christ our Lord.

Gelasian Sacramentary

In the evening

O Lord, who art the shadow of a great rock in a weary land, who beholdest Thy weak creatures weary of labour, weary of pleasures, weary of heart, and weary of self. In Thine abundant compassion and unutterable tenderness bring us, we pray unto Thy rest; through Jesus Christ, Thy Son, our Saviour.

Christina G. Rossetti

Drop Thy still dews of quietness, till all our strivings cease;
Take from our souls the strain and stress,
And let our ordered lives confess the beauty of Thy peace.

Breathe through the heats of our desire Thy coolness and Thy balm;
Let sense be dumb, let flesh retire;
Speak through the earthquake, wind and fire, O still small voice of calm!

John Greenleaf Whittier

DAY 8

Blessed is the man who makes the Lord his trust.

God is our refuge and strength, a very present help in trouble. Therefore we will not fear, even though the earth be removed, and though the mountains be carried into the midst of the sea; though its waters roar and be troubled, though the mountains shake with its swelling. There is a river whose streams shall make glad the city of God, the holy place of the tabernacle of the Most High. God is in the midst of her, she shall not be moved; God shall help her at the break of dawn. The nations raged, the kingdoms were moved; he uttered his voice, the earth melted. The Lord of hosts is with us; the God of Jacob is our refuge. Be still and know that I am God; I will be exalted among the nations, I will be exalted in the earth!

Put thou thy trust in God, in duty's path go on;
Walk in His strength with faith and hope, so shall thy work be done.

Through waves and clouds and storms His power will clear thy way:
Wait thou His time; the darkest night shall end in brightest day.

PRAYERS

In the morning
Safe in the shadow of the Lord beneath his hand and power,
I trust in him, I trust in him, my fortress and my tower.

Strong in the Everlasting Name, and in my Father's care,
I trust in him, I trust in him, who hears and answers prayer.

Safe in the shadow of the Lord, possessed by love divine,
I trust in him, I trust in him, and meet his love with mine.
Timothy Dudley-Smith

Thank you for the assurance of your Word that you never fail those who trust in you.
Help me, I pray, to trust where I cannot see.

In the evening
My hope is set on God alone though Satan spreads his snare,
I trust in him, I trust in him, to keep me in his care.

From fears and phantoms of the night, from foes about my way,
I trust in him, I trust in him, by darkness as by day.

His holy angels keep my feet secure from every stone;
I trust in him, I trust in him, and unafraid go on.
Timothy Dudley-Smith

DAY 9

God is our refuge and strength, an ever-present
help in trouble;
therefore we will not fear.

DAILY READING *From Psalm 27*

The Lord is my light and my salvation; whom shall I fear? The Lord is the strength of my life; of whom shall I be afraid? One thing I have desired of the Lord, that will I seek: that I may dwell in the house of the Lord all the days of my life, to behold the beauty of the Lord and to inquire in his temple. For in the time of trouble he shall hide me in his pavilion; in the secret place of his tabernacle he shall hide me; he shall set me high upon a rock. Wait on the Lord; be of good courage, and he shall strengthen your heart; wait, I say, on the Lord!

He walked where I walk, he stood where I stand,
He felt what I feel, he understands.
He knows my frailty, shared my humanity,
Tempted in every way, yet without sin.

PRAYERS

In the morning

Almighty God, Who seest that we have no power of ourselves to help ourselves; keep us both outwardly in our bodies, and inwardly in our souls; that we may be defended from all adversities which may happen to the body, and from all evil thoughts which may assault and hurt the soul; through Jesus Christ our Lord.

Gregorian Sacramentary

In the evening

Abide with me; fast falls the eventide:
the darkness deepens; Lord, with me abide;
when other helpers fail, and comforts flee,
help of the helpless, O abide with me.

I need Thy presence every passing hour;
what but Thy grace can foil the tempter's power?
Who like Thyself my guide and stay can be?
Through cloud and sunshine, O abide with me.

I fear no foe with Thee at hand to bless;
ills have no weight, and tears no bitterness.
Where is death's sting? Where, grave, thy victory?
I triumph still if Thou abide with me.

Hold Thou Thy cross before my closing eyes,
shine through the gloom, and point me to the skies;
heaven's morning breaks, and earth's vain shadows
flee: in life, in death, O Lord abide with me!

Henry Francis Lyte

DAY 10

This God is our God for ever and ever; he will be our guide even to the end.

DAILY READING *From Psalm 73*

I am always with you; you hold me by my right hand. You guide me with your counsel, and afterwards you will take me into glory. Whom have I in heaven but you? And earth has nothing I desire besides you. My flesh and my heart may fail, but God is the strength of my heart and my portion for ever. Those who are far from you will perish; but as for me, it is good to be near God. I have made the Sovereign Lord my refuge; I will tell of all your deeds.

God holds the key of all unknown, and I am glad:
If other hands should hold the key,
Or if he trusted it to me, I might be sad.

The very dimness of my sight makes me secure;
For, groping in my misty way, I feel his hand;
I hear him say, my help is sure.

PRAYERS

In the morning

O God of Bethel, by whose hand Thy people still are fed,
Who through this weary pilgrimage hast all our fathers led.

Our vows, our prayers, we now present before Thy
throne of grace;
God of our fathers, be the God of their succeeding race.

Through each perplexing path of life our wandering
footsteps guide;
Give us each day our daily bread, and raiment fit provide.

O spread Thy covering wings around, 'til all our
wanderings cease,
And at our Father's loved abode our souls arrive in peace.
Philip Doddridge and John Logan

In the evening

Thou knowest, O Lord, how faint-hearted and discouraged
we often become as we journey along the perplexing pathway
of life. Give unto us, we pray, that spirit of endurance which
shall make us strong in the hour of temptation and enable
us to prevail in times of trial so that by Thy grace we may
go onward until our journeying days are done. This we ask
for Jesus' sake.
W.R.Mackay

Thank you, my Father, for the assurance that you will never
desert me or let me down. You know my weakness and
failure, but I have your totally trustworthy promise that
your strong arm will support me to the end of life's journey.

DAY 11

Cast your burden on the Lord and he will sustain you.

DAILY READING *From Hebrews 4*

Since we have a great high priest who has gone through the heavens, Jesus the Son of God, let us hold firmly to the faith we profess. For we do not have a high priest who is unable to sympathise with our weaknesses, but we have one who has been tempted in every way, just as we are - yet was without sin. Let us then approach the throne of grace with confidence, so that we may receive mercy and find grace to help us in our time of need.

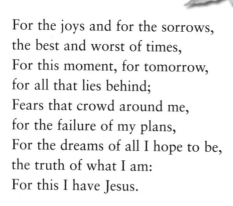

For the joys and for the sorrows,
the best and worst of times,
For this moment, for tomorrow,
for all that lies behind;
Fears that crowd around me,
for the failure of my plans,
For the dreams of all I hope to be,
the truth of what I am:
For this I have Jesus.

PRAYERS

In the morning
O Almighty and merciful Father, Who art the help of the helpless, and the lifter up of the fallen, look down with Thy mercy on all who are oppressed in mind and body; comfort and relieve them, according to their several necessities; give them patience under their sufferings, and a happy issue out of all their afflictions; and this we beg for Jesus Christ's sake. Amen.

Edward Goulburn

Father, I thank you for the assurance that you will indeed sustain those who cast their burdens on you. Help me to do just that - and to leave them with you.

In the evening
Lord, support us all the day long of this troublous life, until the shades lengthen and the evening comes and the busy world is hushed, the fever of life is over and our work is done. Then, Lord, in your mercy grant us safe lodging, a holy rest and peace at the last, through Jesus Christ our Lord.

Cardinal Newman

DAY 12

Whenever I am afraid, I will trust in you.

DAILY READING *From John 14*

Let not your heart be troubled; you believe in God, believe also in me. In my Father's house are many mansions; if it were not so, I would have told you. I go to prepare a place for you. And if I go and prepare a place for you, I will come again and receive you to myself; that where I am you may be also. And where I go you know and the way you know. Thomas said to him, "Lord, we do not know where you are going and how can we know the way?" Jesus said to him, "I am the way, the truth and the life. No-one comes to the Father except through me."

Low at his feet lay thy burden of carefulness
High on his heart he will bear it for thee,
Comfort thy sorrows, and answer thy prayerfulness,
Guiding thy steps as may best for thee be.

PRAYERS

In the morning
I am trusting Thee, Lord Jesus, trusting only Thee;
Trusting Thee for full salvation, great and free.

I am trusting Thee to guide me; Thou alone shalt lead,
Every day and hour supplying all my need.

I am trusting Thee, Lord Jesus; never let me fall;
I am trusting Thee for ever, and for all.

Frances Ridley Havergal

Lord, I confess I am afraid, particularly of ....
Help me to trust you, assured of your promise that you
will never let me down.

In the evening
Be present, O merciful God, and protect us through
the silent hours of this night, so that we who are sick
and weary may rest untroubled and unafraid;
through Jesus Christ our Lord.

Ancient Collect

DAY 13

Bless the Lord O my soul, and forget not
all his benefits.

DAILY READING *From Psalm 107*

Oh, give thanks to the Lord, for he is good! For his mercy endures forever. Let the redeemed of the Lord say so, whom he has redeemed from the hand of the enemy, and gathered out of the lands, from the east and from the west, from the north and from the south. They wandered in the wilderness in a desolate way; they found no city to dwell in. Hungry and thirsty, their soul fainted in them. Then they cried out to the Lord in their trouble, and he delivered them out of their distresses. And he led them by the right way, that they might go to a city for a dwelling place. Oh, that men would give thanks to the Lord for his goodness, and for his wonderful deeds to the children of men! For he satisfies the longing soul, and fills the hungry soul with goodness.

Amazing grace! how sweet the sound that saved a
wretch like me:
I once was lost, but now am found; was blind
but now I see.

The Lord has promised good to me,
his word my hope secures;
He will my shield and portion be as long
as life endures.

PRAYERS

In the morning

When all your mercies, O my God, my thankful soul surveys,
Uplifted by the view, I'm lost in wonder, love, and praise.

Joseph Addison

O Lord, Who though Thou wast rich, yet for our sakes
didst become poor, and has promised in Thy gospel that
whatsoever is done unto the least of Thy brethren, Thou
wilt receive as done unto Thee; give us grace, we humbly
beseech Thee, to be ever willing and ready to minister as
Thou enablest us, to the necessities of our
fellow-creatures, and to extend the blessings of Thy
kingdom over all the world, to Thy praise and glory,
who art God over all, blessed for ever.

St Augustine

In the evening

O God who hast prepared for them that love Thee
such good things as pass man's understanding, pour
into our hearts such love towards Thee, that we,
loving Thee above all things, may obtain Thy
promises, which exceed all that we can desire;
through Jesus Christ our Lord.

Gelasian Sacramentary

DAY 14

We do not know what to do, but our eyes are upon you.

DAILY READING *From Psalm 40*

I waited patiently for the Lord; and he inclined to me and heard my cry. He also brought me up out of a horrible pit, out of the miry clay, and set my feet upon a rock, and established my steps. He has put a new song in my mouth - praise to our God; many will see it and fear and trust in the Lord. Blessed is that man who makes the Lord his trust, who does not respect the proud, nor such as turn aside to lies. Many, O Lord my God, are your wonderful works which you have done; and your thoughts to us cannot be recounted to you in order; if I were I to declare and speak of them, they are more than can be numbered.

I to the hills will lift mine eyes, from whence doth come mine aid?
My safety cometh from the Lord, who heaven and earth hath made.

Thy foot he'll not let slide, nor will he slumber that thee keeps.
Behold, he that keeps Israel, he slumbers not nor sleeps.

PRAYERS

In the morning

We seek a clear light to shine upon our troubled way.
We ask you to give us clearer directions. Where we have
missed the way and wandered far, bring us back, at
whatever cost to our pride. Take away our stubborn
self-will, for we know that in your will alone is our
peace. We seek that peace. We pray in that name which
is above every name, even Jesus Christ our Lord.

Peter Marshall

In the evening

Our gracious God and Father in heaven, you
know the doubts and fears which arise in our minds
from time to time which cause us to lose confidence
both in ourselves and in you. Increase our faith,
O Lord, so that with renewed hope and confidence,
we may rest in your promises and feel assured that
you are with us at all times and in all circumstances.
We ask this in the name and for the sake of
Christ our Saviour.

W.R.MacKay

DAY 15

The Lord is near to all who call on him.

DAILY READING *From Psalm 130*

Out of the depths I cry to you, O Lord; O Lord, hear my voice. Let your ears be attentive to my cry for mercy. If you, O Lord, kept a record of sins, O Lord, who could stand? But with you there is forgiveness; therefore you are feared. I wait for the Lord, my soul waits, and in his word I put my hope. My soul waits for the Lord more than watchmen wait for the morning, more than watchmen wait for the morning.

Down in the human heart, crushed by the tempter,
Feelings lie buried that grace can restore;
Touched by a loving hand, wakened by kindness,
Chords that were broken will vibrate once more.

PRAYERS

In the morning

Eternal and ever blessed God, Who didst bring peace through the blood of Thy Cross, grant that as we journey through this troubled world we may know that deep sweet peace which passes understanding, and even amidst the storms and anxieties of life may we know that all is well if our trust is in Thee. We ask this, with the forgiveness of all our sins, for Christ's sake.

W.R. Mackay

O Lord Jesus, Thou hast invited me "to ask, to seek, to knock" - assuring me that if I ask, it shall be given unto me; if I seek I shall find; if I knock, it shall be opened unto me. Help me to believe that, O God. Give me the faith to ask, knowing that I shall receive. Give me the faith to seek, believing that I shall surely find. Give me the faith and the persistence to knock, knowing that it shall be opened unto me.

Peter Marshall

In the evening

Thank you, O God, for the people who have looked after me to-day, and for those who visited me; for the letters and the get-well cards; for the flowers and gifts friends have sent.

DAY 16

Give thanks to the Lord for he is good. His love endures for ever.

DAILY READING *From Psalm 95*

Oh come, let us sing to the Lord! Let us shout joyfully to the rock of our salvation. Let us come before his presence with thanksgiving; Let us shout joyfully to him with psalms. For the Lord is the great God, and the great king above all gods. In his hand are the deep places of the earth; the heights of the hills are his also. The sea is his, for he made it; and his hands formed the dry land. Oh come, let us worship and bow down; Let us kneel before the Lord our maker. For he is our God, and we are the people of his pasture, and the sheep of his hand.

How good is the God we adore, our faithful, unchangeable Friend!
His love is as great as his power, and knows neither measure nor end!

'Tis Jesus the First and the Last, whose Spirit shall guide us safe home;
We'll praise him for all that is past, we'll trust him for all that's to come.

PRAYERS

In the morning
Thank you, O my Father, for giving us your Son
And leaving your Spirit till the work on earth is done
Melody Green

Help me, dear Lord, to show the fruit of your Spirit in
my life to-day: your love, your joy, your peace, your
patience, your kindness, your goodness, your faithfulness
and your gentleness.

In the evening
Lord, I know you are good. I want to thank you for
being so good to me, in spite of my insignificance
and sinfulness. And I thank you for the assurance
that your love endures for ever.

Father, I give you thanks for all those times when
you have been with me in moments of weakness and
suffering. More than ever before, your love seemed
all about me and beneath me. I remember with
gratitude the encouragement of friends and the care
of those who were closest to me. May the
remembrance of your goodness fill all the coming
days with confidence and with hope.
Michael Walker

DAY 17

Let him who walks in the dark, who has no light, trust in the name of the Lord.

DAILY READING *From Habakkuk 3*

Though the fig-tree does not bud and there are no grapes on the vines, though the olive crop fails and the fields produce no food, though there are no sheep in the pen and no cattle in the stalls, yet I will rejoice in the Lord, I will be joyful in God my Saviour. The Sovereign Lord is my strength; he makes my feet like the feet of a deer, he enables me to go on the heights.

I am not skilled to understand what God has willed, what God has planned;
I only know at his right hand stands One who is my Saviour.

PRAYERS

In the morning
Thy way, not mine, O Lord, however dark it be;
Lead me by Thine own hand, choose out the path for me.

Smooth let it be or rough, it will be still the best;
Winding or straight, it leads right onward to Thy rest.

I dare not choose my lot; I would not if I might:
Choose Thou for me, my God, so shall I walk aright.

Horatius Bonar

Lord, I am walking in the dark, just now. My future is
obscure. Help me to trust you completely.

In the evening
I know that sleep is one of the best medicines for both
the body and the mind. Help me to sleep tonight. Into
your strong hands I place all those away from their
own home, the night staff caring for them, my loved
ones, whose names I now mention, and myself with my
fears, my worries and my hopes. Help me to sleep,
thinking of you and your promises.

O most merciful Redeemer, Friend and Brother, may I
know Thee more clearly,
Love Thee more dearly, follow more nearly; for ever
and ever, Amen.

Richard of Chichester

DAY 18

I have loved you with an everlasting love.

DAILY READING *From Romans 8*

We know that all things work together for good to those who love God, to those who are the called according to his purpose. What then shall we say to these things? If God is for us who can be against us? He who did not spare his own Son, but delivered him up for us all, how shall he not with him also freely give us all things? Who shall separate us from the love of Christ? Shall tribulation or distress or persecution or famine or nakedness or peril or sword? Yet in all these things we are more than conquerors through him who loved us. For I am persuaded that neither death nor life, nor angels nor principalities, nor powers, nor things present nor things to come, nor height nor depth, nor any other created thing shall be able to separate us from the love of God which is in Christ Jesus our Lord.

Loved with everlasting love,
Led by grace that love to know;
Spirit, breathing from above,
Thou hast taught me it is so.
O this full and perfect peace!
O this transport all divine!
In a love which cannot cease,
I am His and He is mine.

PRAYERS

In the morning
I do need you. Lord, I need you now. I know that I can
do without many of the things that once I thought were
necessities, but without you I cannot live, and dare not
die. I needed you when sorrow came, when shadows
were thrown across the threshold of my life, and you did
not fail me then. I know that I need you even in the
sunshine, and shall still need you tomorrow. I thank you
for that constant sense of need that keeps me close to
your side. Help me to keep my hand in yours and my
ears open to the wisdom of your voice. Speak to me, that
I may hear you giving me courage for hard times and
strength for difficult places. I ask for no easy way, but
just your grace that is sufficient for every need.

From Peter Marshall

In the evening
Help me, O Lord, to commit my suffering, my
weakness, my depression to you, and grant me the
grace of acceptance and patience if immediate relief
is not your good and perfect will. Thank you for the
assurance that nothing is too hard for you.

O Love that wilt not let me go, I rest my weary soul
in Thee:
I give Thee back the life I owe, that in Thine ocean
depths its flow may richer, fuller be.

George Matheson

DAY 19

The Lord is good, a refuge in times of trouble.
He cares for those who trust in him.

DAILY READING *From Luke 15*

Now the tax collectors and 'sinners' were all gathering round to hear him. But the Pharisees and the teachers of the law muttered, "This man welcomes sinners, and eats with them." Then Jesus told them this parable: "Suppose one of you has a hundred sheep and loses one of them. Does he not leave the ninety-nine in the open country and go after the lost sheep until he finds it? And when he finds it, he joyfully puts it on his shoulders and goes home. Then he calls his friends and neighbours together and says, 'Rejoice with me; I have found my lost sheep.' I tell you that in the same way there will be more rejoicing in heaven over one sinner who repents than over ninety-nine righteous persons who do not need to repent."

There is no place where earth's sorrows are more felt than up in heaven:
There is no place where earth's failings have such kindly judgment given.

For the love of God is broader than the measures of man's mind;
And the heart of the Eternal is most wonderfully kind.

PRAYERS

In the morning
Lord, I thank you that you have shown yourself to be a refuge to countless generations of your people. You have never failed any of your children, and I know that you will not fail me.

O God, help me to live today well. Help me to bear pain, if need be, uncomplainingly and discomfort cheerfully. Help me to cause as little trouble and to give as much help as possible. And help me today to take one step forward on the road back to health and serenity. This I ask for Jesus' sake.

From William Barclay

In the evening
Jesu, Lover of my soul, let me to Thy bosom fly,
While the nearer waters roll, while the tempest still is high;
Hide me, O my Saviour, hide till the storm of life be past;
Safe into the haven guide, O receive my soul at last.

Other refuge have I none, hangs my helpless soul on Thee;
Leave, ah! leave me not alone, still support and comfort me;
All my trust on Thee is stayed, all my help from Thee I bring;
Cover my defenceless head with the shadow of Thy wing.

Charles Wesley

DAY 20

I will never turn away anyone who comes to me.

DAILY READING *From Psalm 51*

Have mercy on me, O God, according to your unfailing love; according to your great compassion blot out my transgressions. Wash away all my iniquity and cleanse me from my sin. Cleanse me with hyssop, and I will be clean; wash me, and I will be whiter than snow. Let me hear joy and gladness; let the bones you have crushed rejoice. Hide your face from my sins and blot out all my iniquity. Create in me a pure heart, O God, and renew a steadfast spirit within me. Do not cast me from your presence or take your Holy Spirit from me. Restore to me the joy of your salvation and grant me a willing spirit to sustain me. O Lord, open my lips, and my mouth will declare your praise.

Before the throne of God above I have a strong, a perfect plea,
A great High Priest whose name is Love, who ever lives and pleads for me.
My name is graven on his hands, my name is written on his heart;
I know that while in heaven he stands no power can force me to depart.

PRAYERS

In the morning
Lord Jesus, I pray for an ability to grasp the truth of your promise that you will never turn away anyone who comes to you; that through believing in you eternal life is given as a present possession, and that your sheep are totally and everlastingly secure. I pray that I may be able to re-affirm my faith in you, even if it means saying: "Lord, I believe; help my unbelief."

My faith looks up to Thee, Thou Lamb of Calvary,
Saviour divine:
Now hear me while I pray; take all my guilt away;
O let me from this day be wholly Thine.
Ray Palmer

In the evening
Father, I have lost the feeling of your presence. Yet deep in my heart, I know it is not because you have left me, but because I have wandered from you. My heart is sick of being lost. I want to return to you now, and to be led in your way. O my Father receive me, your prodigal child. I arise and come back to you, my Father, knowing that you are even now running to meet me, placing over my shoulders the robe of your love - a love which loved me while I was yet a sinner - a love that brought Jesus to Calvary. I thank you for that love.

From Peter Marshall

DAY 21

You do not realise now what I am doing, but later you will understand.

DAILY READING *From Isaiah 55*

Come, all you who are thirsty, come to the waters; and you who have no money come buy and eat! Come, buy wine and milk without money and without cost. Seek the Lord while he may be found; call on him while he is near. Let the wicked forsake his way, and the evil man his thoughts. Let him turn to the Lord and he will have mercy on him, and to our God, for he will freely pardon. For my thoughts are not your thoughts, neither are your ways my ways declares the Lord. As the heavens are higher than the earth, so are my ways higher than your ways and my thoughts than your thoughts.

God moves in a mysterious way, his wonders
to perform;
He plants his footsteps in the sea, and rides
upon the storm.

Deep in unfathomable mines of never-failing skill,
He treasures up his bright designs, and works
his sovereign will.

PRAYERS

In the morning

O Thou most holy and loving God, we thank Thee once more for the quiet rest of the night that has gone by, for the new promise that has come with this fresh morning, and for the hope of this day. While we have slept, the world in which we live has swept on as we have rested under the shadow of Thy love. May we trust Thee this day for all the needs of the body, the soul and the spirit. Amen.

Robert Collyer

Deep down, I realise that your way is perfect, but my puny mind cannot understand the reason for all your actions. Please help me to trust when I cannot see.

In the evening

O Almighty God who alone canst order the unruly wills and affections of sinful men; grant unto Thy people that they may love the thing which Thou commandest, and desire that which Thou dost promise; so that, among the sundry and manifold changes of this world, our hearts may be fixed where true joys are to be found; through Jesus Christ our Lord.

Galasian Sacramentary

DAY 22

Thou dost keep him in perfect peace, whose mind is stayed on thee.

DAILY READING *From Psalm 62*

My soul, wait silently for God alone, for my expectation is from him. He only is my rock and my salvation; he is my defence; I shall not be moved. In God is my salvation and my glory; the rock of my strength, and my refuge is in God. Trust in him at all times, you people; pour out your heart before him; God is a refuge for us. Truly my soul silently waits for God; from him comes my salvation.

Peace, perfect peace, in this dark world of sin?
The blood of Jesus whispers peace within.

Peace, perfect peace, with loved ones far away?
In Jesus' keeping we are safe and they.

Peace, perfect peace, our future all unknown?
Jesus we know, and he is on the throne.

PRAYERS

In the morning
Father,
I place into your hands my friends and family; for I
know I always can trust you.

Jenny Hewer *

Father, I am so grateful for the realisation that you know
all about my loved ones and their needs and their
situation at this very moment. I thank you that all that
you do is guided by your infinite wisdom, love and
power. I place them confidently in your hands.

In the evening
My times are in Thy hand: My God, I wish them there;
My life, my friends, my soul, I leave entirely to Thy care.

My times are in Thy hand, whatever they may be,
Pleasing or painful, dark or bright, as best may seem
to Thee.

My times are in Thy hand, Jesus, the crucified;
Those hands my cruel sins had pierced are now my
guard and guide.

My times are in Thy hand: I'll always trust in Thee;
And, after death, at Thy right hand, I shall forever be.

William Freeman Lloyd

*Extract taken from the song "Father, I place into your hands" by
Jenny Hewer. Copyright (c) 1975 Thankyou Music

DAY 23

We know that all things work together for good to those who love God.

DAILY READING *From Ephesians 1*

Blessed be the God and Father of our Lord Jesus Christ, who has blessed us with every spiritual blessing in the heavenly places in Christ, just as he chose us in him before the foundation of the world, that we should be holy and without blame before him in love, having predestined us to adoption as sons by Jesus Christ to himself, according to the good pleasure of his will, to the praise of the glory of his grace, by which he made us accepted in the Beloved. In him we have redemption through his blood, the forgiveness of sins, according to the riches of his grace which he made to abound toward us in all wisdom and prudence.

All the way my Saviour leads me; what have I to ask beside?
Can I doubt his tender mercy, who through life has
been my guide?
Heavenly peace, divinest comfort, here by faith in him to dwell!
For I know whate'er befall me, Jesus doeth all things well.

All the way my Saviour leads me, O the fullness of his love!
Perfect rest to me is promised in my Father's house above.
When my spirit, clothed, immortal, wings its flight to
realms of day,
This, my song through endless ages: Jesus led me all the way!

PRAYERS

In the morning
Father, help me drop my anchor into the depths of this
reassuring and encouraging revelation: that nothing that
ever happens to me is beyond your power to transform.
Every stumbling block becomes a stepping stone.
I am so grateful. Amen.

Selwyn Hughes

Thou hast made us for Thyself, O Lord, and our hearts
are restless until they find rest in Thee. Grant us, we
pray: in all our duties, Thy help;
in all our perplexities, Thy guidance;
in all our dangers, Thy protection;
in all our sorrows, Thy peace;
through Jesus Christ, our Lord, Amen.

St Augustine

In the evening
Jesus, Thou joy of loving hearts,
Thou fount of life, Thou Light of men,
From the best bliss that earth imparts,
We turn unfilled to Thee again.

Our restless spirits yearn for Thee,
Where'er our changeful lot is cast:
Glad, when Thy gracious smile we see;
Blest, when our faith can hold Thee fast.

Bernard of Clairvaux
(Translated by Ray Palmer)

DAY 24

God is faithful; he will not let you be tempted beyond what you can bear.

DAILY READING *From Ephesians 6*

Be strong in the Lord and in his mighty power. Put on the full armour of God so that you can take your stand against the devil's schemes. For our struggle is not against flesh and blood, but against the rulers, against the authorities, against the powers of this dark world and against the spiritual forces of evil in the heavenly realms. Therefore put on the full armour of God, so that when the day of evil comes, you may be able to stand your ground, and after you have done everything to stand. Take the helmet of salvation and the sword of the Spirit, which is the word of God. And pray in the Spirit on all occasions with all kinds of prayers and requests. With this in mind, be alert and always keep on praying for all the saints.

And when the strife is fierce, the warfare long,
Steals on the ear the distant triumph song,
And hearts are brave again, and arms are strong.
Hallelujah!

PRAYERS

In the morning

My God, I thank you for your faithfulness. You never let down those who trust in you. I thank you too for your promise that you will not let us be tempted beyond what we can bear. And you know my limits; you know that I cannot bear much.

Faithful One, so unchanging;
ageless One, you're my rock of peace.
Lord of all, I depend on you, I call out to you again and again.
You are my rock in times of trouble,
You lift me up when I fall down;
all through the storm, Your love is the anchor -
my hope is in You alone.

Brian Doerksen

In the evening

We thank Thee, O God, for those who have travelled over the tempestuous seas of this life and have made the harbour of peace and felicity. Watch over us, who are still on our dangerous voyage: and remember such as lie exposed to the rough storms of trouble and temptation. Frail is our vessel and the ocean is wide: but in Thy mercy Thou hast set our course, so steer the vessel of our life toward the everlasting shore of peace, and bring us at length to the quiet haven of our heart's desire, where Thou, O our God, art blessed and livest and reignest for ever and ever. Amen.

St. Augustine

DAY 25

How can I repay the Lord for all his goodness to me?

DAILY READING *From Psalms 103*

Bless the Lord, O my soul; and all that is within me, bless his holy name!
Bless the Lord, O my soul, and forget not all his benefits: who forgives all your iniquities, who heals all your diseases, who redeems your life from destruction, who crowns you with loving kindness and tender mercies. The Lord is merciful and gracious, slow to anger, and abounding in mercy. He has not dealt with us according to our sins, nor punished us according to our iniquities. For as the heavens are high above the earth, so great is his mercy toward those who fear him.

Praise, my soul, the King of heaven;
to his feet thy tribute bring;
Ransomed, healed, restored, forgiven,
who like me his praise should sing?
Praise him! Praise him! Praise him! Praise him!
Praise the everlasting King.

PRAYERS

In the morning

O Lord, in whose hands are life and death, by whose power I am sustained, and by whose mercy I am spared, look down upon me with pity. Forgive me that I have until now so much neglected the duty which Thou hast assigned to me, and suffered the days and hours of which I must give account to pass away without any endeavour to accomplish Thy will. Make me to remember, O God, that every day is Thy gift, and ought to be used according to Thy command. Grant me, therefore, so to repent of my negligence, that I may obtain mercy from Thee, and pass the time which Thou shalt yet allow me in diligent performance of Thy commands; through Jesus Christ our Lord.

Samuel Johnson

In the evening

Great is Thy faithfulness, O God my Father,
There is no shadow of turning with Thee;
Thou changest not, Thy compassions they fail not,
As Thou hast been Thou for ever wilt be.

Thomas O. Chisholm

DAY 26

My grace is sufficient for you, for my power is made perfect in weakness.

By faith Jacob, when he was dying, blessed each of Joseph's sons, and worshipped as he leaned on the top of his staff.... I do not have time to tell about Gideon, Barak, Samson, Jepthah, David, Samuel and the prophets, who through faith conquered kingdoms, administered justice, and gained what was promised; who shut the mouths of lions, quenched the fury of the flames, and escaped the edge of the sword: whose weakness was turned to strength. Without faith it is impossible to please God, because anyone who comes to him must believe that he exists and that he rewards those who earnestly seek him.

How sweet the name of Jesus sounds in
a believer's ear!
It soothes his sorrows, heals his wounds,
and drives away his fear.

It makes the wounded spirit whole,
and calms the troubled breast;
It satisfies the hungry soul, and gives the weary rest.

Weak is the effort of my heart,
and cold my warmest thought;
But when I see you as you are, I'll praise you as I ought.

PRAYERS

In the morning

Lord, you know my weakness just now. Thank you that your grace is sufficient for my need and that, amazingly, your power shows up best in those who are weak.

O God, the Father of lights, from whom cometh down every good and perfect gift, have mercy on our frailty, and grant us such health of body as Thou knowest to be needful for us; that both in our bodies and our souls we may evermore serve Thee with all our strength and might; through Jesus Christ our Lord. Amen.

Bishop Cosin

In the evening

What a good and bountiful God you are, O Lord; and how good you have been to me.
I particularly want to thank you for helping me to-day when I had problems and cares which seemed insoluble.

DAY 27

God is able to do so much more than we can ever ask for, or even think of, by means of the power working in us.

DAILY READING *From Ephesians 3*

I kneel before the Father, from whom his whole family in heaven and on earth derives its name. I pray that out of his glorious riches he may strengthen you with power through his Spirit in your inner being, so that Christ may dwell in your hearts through faith. And I pray that you, being rooted and established in love, may have power, together with all the saints, to grasp how wide and long and high and deep is the love of Christ, and to know this love that surpasses knowledge - that you may be filled to the measure of all the fulness of God.

Cast care aside, lean on your Guide,
His boundless mercy will provide;
Trust, and your trusting soul shall prove,
Christ is its life and Christ its love.

Faint not, nor fear, his arm is near;
He does not change and you are dear,
Only believe, and Christ shall be your all in all eternally.

Yesterday, today, for ever, Jesus is the same;
All may change, but Jesus never, glory to his name!

PRAYERS

In the morning
Eternal God, we rejoice in your promise that as our day
is, so shall our strength be; and we ask your help for all
who are old and wearied with the burden of life. In your
strength may they find courage and peace; and in their
advancing years may they learn more of your love;
through Jesus Christ our Lord.

New Every Morning

Lord, I thank you for reminding me of your infinite
power. Truly, 'There is nothing too hard for the Lord.'
Thank you that this power works in your children and
that you surprise us by doing more than we ask or
imagine to be possible.

In the evening
Lord, I come to you in penitence, in trust, in hope:
I come praising your glorious name.
Heal every part of me, in body, in mind, in spirit.
Save me from all evil.
For I long to serve you, in joy, in peace and in
power, and to praise you all my days.

John Gunstone

DAY 28

I have the strength to face all conditions by the power that Christ gives me.

I will extol the Lord at all times; his praise will always be on my lips. My soul will boast in the Lord; let the afflicted hear and rejoice. Glorify the Lord with me: let us exalt his name together. I sought the Lord and he answered me; he delivered me from all my fears. Those who look to him are radiant; their faces are never covered with shame. The angel of the Lord encamps around those who fear him and he delivers them. Taste and see that the Lord is good; blessed is the man who takes refuge in him. The righteous cry out, and the Lord hears them; he delivers them from all their troubles. The Lord is close to the broken-hearted and saves those who are crushed in spirit. A righteous man may have many troubles, but the Lord delivers him from them all.

I'll go in the strength of the Lord, in paths he has marked for my feet;
I'll follow the light of his word, nor shrink from the dangers I meet.
His presence my steps shall attend, his fullness my wants shall supply;
On him, 'til my journey shall end, my unwavering faith will rely.

PRAYERS

In the morning

Lord, we know not what a day may bring forth. There are hours ahead which raise doubts and fears in my mind. I thank you for the assurance that in the Lord Jesus Christ you give me the strength to face the worst that may happen. When I am slighted and misunderstood, help me to be forgiving, remembering how much I have needed and been granted your forgiveness.

Father, give to us and to all your people, in times of anxiety, serenity; in times of hardship, courage; in times of uncertainty, patience; and at all times, a quiet trust in your wisdom and love; through Jesus Christ our Lord.

New Every Morning

In the evening

Teach us, good Lord,
to serve Thee as Thou deservest;
to give and not to count the cost;
to fight and not to heed the wounds;
to toil and not to seek for rest;
to labour and not to ask for any reward,
save that of knowing that we do Thy will. Amen.

Ignatius Loyola

DAY 29

If any of you lacks wisdom, let him ask of God, who gives to all liberally and without reproach, and it will be given to him. But let him ask in faith, with no doubting.

DAILY READING *From Psalm 25*

To you, O Lord, I lift up my soul; in you I trust, O my God. Do not let me be put to shame, nor let my enemies triumph over me. No-one whose hope is in you will ever be put to shame. Show me your ways, O Lord, teach me your paths; guide me in your truth and teach me, for you are God my Saviour, and my hope is in you all day long. Remember, O Lord, your great mercy and love, for they are from of old. Remember not the sins of my youth and my rebellious ways; according to your love remember me, for you are good, O Lord. Good and upright is the Lord; therefore he instructs sinners in his ways. He guides the humble in what is right and teaches them his way. All the ways of the Lord are loving and faithful for those who keep the demands of his covenant.

I've found a friend; O such a friend!
so kind, and true, and tender!
So wise a counsellor and guide, so mighty a defender!
From him who loves me now so well
what power my soul shall sever?
Shall life or death? Shall earth or hell?
No! I am his forever.

PRAYERS

In the morning

O Lord, our heavenly Father, almighty and everlasting God, Who hast safely brought us to the beginning of this day; defend us in the same with Thy mighty power, and grant that this day we fall into no sin, neither run into any kind of danger; but that all our doings may be ordered by Thy governance, to do always that which is righteous in Thy sight; through Jesus Christ our Lord. Amen.

Gelasian Sacramentary

Thank you, Lord, for the wonderful promise that you will give us all the wisdom we need if we ask for it in faith. Help me to pray and not doubt at all.

In the evening

Grant us Thy peace, Lord, through the coming night,
Turn Thou for us its darkness into light;
From harm and danger keep Thy children free,
For dark and light are both alike to Thee.

John Ellerton

DAY 30

Unload all your worries on him, since he is looking after you.

DAILY READING *From Philippians 4*

Rejoice in the Lord always. I will say it again: Rejoice! Let your gentleness be evident to all. The Lord is near. Do not be anxious about anything, but in everything, by prayer and petition, with thanksgiving, present your requests to God. And the peace of God which transcends all understanding will guard your hearts and your minds in Christ Jesus. Finally, brothers, whatever is true, whatever is noble, whatever is right, whatever is pure, whatever is lovely, whatever is admirable - if anything is excellent or praiseworthy - think about such things. Whatever you have learned or received or heard from me, or seen in me - put it into practice and the God of peace will be with you.

In heavenly love abiding, no change my heart shall fear;
And safe is such confiding, for nothing changes here;
The storm may roar without me, my heart may low be laid;
But God is round about me, and can I be dismayed?

Wherever he may guide me, no want shall turn me back;
My Shepherd is beside me, and nothing can I lack;
His wisdom ever waketh, his sight is never dim;
He knows the way he taketh, and I will walk with him.

PRAYERS

In the morning
Through this world of toils and snares, if I falter, Lord,
who cares?
Who with me my burden shares? None but Thee, dear
Lord, none but Thee.

Just a closer walk with Thee, grant it Jesus, this my plea;
Daily walking close with Thee, let it be, dear Lord, let it be.

Anon

Thank you, Lord, for the assurance that you are looking
after me. I find this so amazing, because I often go for
long periods without thinking about you. Help me to do
as your Word exhorts, and unload all my worries on you.

In the evening
O Lord God, in whom we live and move and have our
being, open our eyes that we may behold Thy Fatherly
presence ever about us. Draw our hearts to Thee with
the power of Thy love. Teach us to be anxious for
nothing, and when we have done what Thou hast
given us to do, help us, O God our Saviour, to leave
the issue to Thy wisdom. Take from us all doubt and
mistrust. Lift our thoughts up to Thee and make us to
know that all things are possible to us through Thy
Son our Redeemer. Amen.

Bishop Westcott

DAY 31

If we confess our sins, he will forgive us.

DAILY READING *From Psalm 32*

Blessed is he whose transgressions are forgiven, whose sins are covered. Blessed is the man whose sin the Lord does not count against him and in whose spirit is no deceit. When I kept silent, my bones wasted away through my groaning all day long. For day and night your hand was heavy upon me; my strength was sapped as in the heat of summer. Then I acknowledged my sin to you and did not cover up my iniquity. I said, "I will confess my transgressions to the Lord" and you forgave the guilt of my sin.

Just as I am without one plea, but that thy blood was shed for me,
And that Thou bidd'st me come to Thee,
O Lamb of God, I come.

Just as I am, and waiting not to rid my soul of one dark blot,
To Thee, whose blood can cleanse each spot,
O Lamb of God, I come.

Just as I am, Thou wilt receive, wilt welcome, pardon, cleanse, relieve;
Because Thy promise I believe,
O Lamb of God, I come.

PRAYERS

In the morning

Have mercy upon me, O God, according to your loving kindness; according to the multitude of your tender mercies, blot out my transgressions. Create in me a clean heart, O God, and renew a steadfast spirit within me. Restore to me the joy of your salvation and uphold me by your generous Spirit. O Lord, open my lips, and my mouth shall show forth your praise.

Psalm 51

O the joy of your forgiveness, slowly sweeping over me;
Now in heartfelt adoration, this praise I'll bring to you, my King; I'll worship you, my Lord.

Dave Bilbrough *

In the evening

Rock of ages, cleft for me, let me hide myself in Thee;
Let the water and the blood, from Thy riven side which flowed,
Be of sin the double cure, cleanse me from its guilt and power.

Nothing in my hand I bring, simply to Thy cross I cling;
Naked, come to Thee for dress, helpless, look to Thee for grace;
Foul, I to the fountain fly; wash me, Saviour, or I die.

Augustus Montagu Toplady

Make my heart warm and soft, that I may receive and accept now the blessing of Thy forgiveness, the benediction of Thy "Depart in peace... and sin no more." In Jesus' name.

From Peter Marshall

* Copyright (c) Thankyou Music

WHERE TO FIND HELP FOR SPECIFIC NEEDS